TAKE HEED

Journeying in the Supernatural-Vol. 1

Take Heed
Journeying in the Supernatural–Volume 1
Copyright © 2020 by Austin Campo

Additional copies may be ordered from the publisher for educational,
business, promotional or premium use.
For information, contact ALIVE Book Publishing at:
alivebookpublishing.com, or call (925) 837-7303.

ISBN 13
978-1-63132-111-5

Library of Congress Control Number: 2020922066

Library of Congress Cataloging-in-Publication Data
is available upon request.

First Edition

Published in the United States of America by ALIVE Book Publishing
and ALIVE Publishing Group, imprints of Advanced Publishing LLC
3200 A Danville Blvd., Suite 204, Alamo, California 94507
alivebookpublishing.com

PRINTED IN THE UNITED STATES OF AMERICA

10 9 8 7 6 5 4 3 2 1

TAKE HEED

Journeying in the Supernatural-Vol. 1

Austin Campo

ABOOKS

Alive Book Publishing

FOREWORD

But as it is written:

Eye has not seen, nor ear has heard, nor have entered into the heart of man the things which God has prepared for those that love Him.
~ I Corinthians 2:9 NKJV

I'm not sure I'd taken in the gravity of that thought fully though, 'til July of 2016. The truth was, the supernatural had long been part of my life. It was just brilliantly highlighted that day, and my life has never been the same.

CHAPTER ONE

A Ride into the Unexpected

Heading north and cruising through Alabama, the sun was shining and the temperature was perfect. It was July 5, 2016. I'd been intermittently praying or praising God from the back of the bike since we left. Vacation, now on the downhill slide, couldn't darken this day. It was beautiful!

At one point I shut my eyes and started praising God again, praising Him for everything. Then it happened. It was like in my mind's eye it suddenly looked like I could clearly see a flat solid rock path before me, and a cave opening at the other end. The moment my thoughts grasped what I was seeing, He appeared. It was the Lion of Judah! He walked right out of the cave toward me, in the form of a lion. It was just me looking at Him, and Him looking intently at me.

He made no sound and either did I. There was a certain awe to the moment. To be honest, I don't think I could have said a thing! After a moment or two, He simply turned and went back into the cave and out of sight. I sat for a moment just looking at the cave opening and feeling a mix of awe, fear, and excitement, which seemed all mingled together like some strange ball in my stomach. To this day I'm still not sure how I even knew it was Him.

As I felt then, and said before and after, "I just knew. I just knew." Now, even typing this, I realize *I just knew*, simply because He wanted me to know. I was so excited! I was praising again, out loud now. I kept telling Him, and the angels or whoever was listening, just how awesome He was!

A little later, wide-eyed under my sunglasses, and still on the road, I was looking around the passing scenery. The Alabama countryside was beautiful that day! Up to my right, I saw a big airplane. It seemed like it was flying low. My eyes were drawn to it. It seemed so low, yet not landing. I think I even nudged my husband and tried to point it out. He glanced but we were riding, and on the highway, so there was no conversation. I looked again. I thought, "Boy that sure seems low," and I started praying.

Then, as if I'd been lifted, I found myself in the air and soon right up near the plane, toward the tail end. I could see the whole left side! The plane was a large one. It was white and its logo had a pattern in blue and burnt orange, almost giving a geometric shape with the windows incorporated. I could not see the name of the airline or maybe wasn't allowed to see. Again, just as the Lion of Judah, I heard nothing, not even the plane. No one said anything. If the angels had me, I could not see them. It felt like my eyes were drawn again though, by something other than me, to take in all the details.

Just as sudden, I remembered or was reminded, that I was on the back of the bike. This was a shocking revelation to me! At that moment I guess I also realized I must be in the spirit, or my spirit was in the air, but either way, my body must still be on the bike! Then just like that, so was the rest of me.

Immediately I went on a trail of questions! For a bit, none were answered. When He gave me no answers, I tried to let it go. It didn't last too long, but I didn't want to weary the Lord. So instead, I looked at the passing towns and rural areas as we rode on, and I prayed silently.

I'd kind of let it go eventually. I mean, I wasn't letting it go, I just had let it go for a little while. Then I made one last remark. Something made me tell Him that if He wanted to show me anything further, I wanted to see, but if not, I would leave it alone.

I had my eyes shut right then, but immediately it was bright and sunshiny in my mind's eye. I saw the plane again. This time it was from a distance again, like the start. I was watching and I saw it go down. I mean it dropped low, and then disappeared altogether. Oh my gosh, my heart fell with it! Right then all I can say is I went into a bantering, fervent prayer in English and in tongues, while intermittently quizzing God repeatedly about what plane. What country's plane was it? How many people were on it, and what happened to them? What was the name of the airline? On and on I went, snotting and crying and then feeling undeniably frustrated and concerned all at the same time! I felt such anguish.

When I had run out of words and my heart was just quiet and heavy inside, I asked God if this was or was to be. My main reason was that I wanted to intercede as best I could if it had not happened yet. I thought when we stopped, I'd call some others who would storm heaven with prayers as well. No answer to that question ever came.

As I sat and grieved almost, He showed me the plane again, but this time, from above. Wherever it was, it was very bright and sunshiny, almost seemed kind-of tropical. It seemed like it was sitting in water in a cove. It was land, a plane in water, land again. The water was almost half-way up the plane, but it was not covered. I could feel my insides getting more curious and feel a little bit of hope rising. It was like, without words, asking God about the people, noting that it looked like they could have lived.

Immediately and very clearly, it's as if He took me down. It was as if I was moving down and hovering above the land area left of the plane, and I saw people. I saw a lot of people! It was like some weird single file parade, people of all ages, heights, and color, in a wide array of clothes. Some were wearing shorts and flip flops. Some seemed more in business attire. Others just seemed to be in casual wear. A few had beach-type hats. A few were carrying children. There were also children walking with what must have been a parent. They looked tired, and no one was smiling, but they looked fine, alive.

Now I find myself standing on the land to the left of that plane. My gaze looked down. Part of the land seemed like dirt and some a dirt and sand mix. Just off what would be the beach area, there was a big stone wall that went up, up, up. When I looked up, I realized there was land up on top. Then I realized the stone wall was like a giant retaining wall, though it looked natural. On one part of the stone wall, more toward the water, another stone wall was standing quite tall and running parallel to it. Then I realized the people I saw were walking single file into the crack between the two.

I'm not sure how, but I suddenly seemed to be viewing from inside on the other end, but further in, so I could watch them walking toward me. There were 2-6 inches of water they were moving through inside the space between the two rock walls. It seemed like it was maybe 10-12 ft wide, but they were still just walking single file, and silent.

That day, and for two solid weeks, I talked to people, I prayed, I asked God stuff about it, and I looked up so many airlines that I should have been seeing planes in my sleep! For a long time after that, I had a hard time leaving it alone, but eventually, I had no choice.

Unfortunately, I saw no more about that plane. Nothing was explained. I asked a lot of questions, but honestly, I have gotten no real answers to convey to anyone. The closest I felt I might have come, was that missing Malaysia flight M370 coming to mind a couple of times. It was the one they never found. I looked up what the plane should have looked like, but I never saw it or any other that looked like the one I saw. Had it been that airplane, it could have only been one of two things. It would have had to make an emergency landing in some remote place and just was never found, or someone took the plane and them. I just will not let myself dwell on that side.

It was the last time I saw the plane, the people, or the plight that I encountered. It was the last time God showed me anyway. I have thought of it many times over these last years. I am not sure why He so far has not given me a definitive answer. I guess I accept that maybe it is not for me to know or understand yet. Or perhaps it is a lesson in trying to train me in the gifts He's given me. I let it go to God's sovereignty and His timing.

One thing is for sure, July 5th, 2016, ended up being a roller-coaster of emotions. It also proved to be a pinnacle day of a great change in my life. I didn't know then what I have learned since that time, but for me everything changed that day. He opened my eyes in a way I had not seen before, and the call He told me about nearly seven years before was in the horizon ahead of me.

CHAPTER TWO

The Seeing of it All

The trip back to Ohio was uneventful. I couldn't think of much except the plane, the people, and generally just the wonder of it all. Every stop we made for gas, and one stay overnight, as I said before, I was just busy looking up airlines.

I don't remember saying anything about what I'd seen to our friends, but that would have been about standard for me at that time. I know I did say something to my husband, but can't remember now if it was on the road, or simply when I got home and was still looking up airlines trying to find a picture that matched the plane I'd seen.

My not speaking out what I was seeing then was likely part being overwhelmed myself, and because I had seen a lot up to that point for years, but had learned to be careful what or how I relay it to people. By then, I didn't share anything without being directed by Holy Spirit, or by asking and being given permission.

I had both shared much and held back much with my husband by that point. He believed. He'd accepted Jesus years before, but the things I was normally shown made him uncomfortable. He'd say things like, "If He shows you anything about me, don't tell me," or "I don't want to know the future. I'd rather just see it when we get there." I know his words rang in my heart a few times because sometimes I didn't want to see what I was seeing either! Outside of his not wanting to know though, I think sometimes he was teetering between being uncomfortable with hearing such things, and just thinking I was crazy.

As per usual, when he hit the 270-outer belt, we split from the friends we were riding back with. They went one way and we went the other. Then before I knew it, we were home, just like magic. Very quickly after, I realized I didn't remember much of the scenery from Alabama on. My being preoccupied is probably a dramatic understatement! My mind was trying to wrap around it all. Though I had experienced God's supernatural side leading up to this, it was the way I was now *"seeing,"* both eyes shut, and eyes open. That was different.

I never had a lot of visions. Usually, I had what I called "God dreams". I'd had them for years. I had only one major vision to that point that showed a future cataclysmic event, and two significant ones. One was of a personal nature and another announced my future call. We'll talk about those two sometime later. Outside of that, I'd had small ones here and there for intercession purposes. To that point, visions for me probably could have been counted on a little more than two hands.

I used to joke with my believing friends that I knew He had to give me dreams because my mind was so cluttered with everything during the day, He had to wait until I was in a dead sleep to get my attention! I joked with them, which usually made them laugh, but to be honest, it was probably the truth.

Being home felt strange. Just a couple of days before, I was sewing up a trip in the sun, riding on the back of a motorcycle, sharing meals and great times with my honey and friends. Then I was thrust unexpectedly into the supernatural side of God, and had my eyes opened in a way I had not quite encountered 'til then.

Now was it all just supposed to go back to normal? How could I be normal? I mean, I knew work was waiting for me to come back, chores were still going to be there. Regular life was there waiting for me. I just didn't feel the same, and I suppose something deep inside me was telling me it never would *be* the same. *I* would never be the same.

As you might imagine, life did go on, and I settled in it as best I could. My new normal had me seeking Him even more, and even more greatly looking forward to the times where I could purposely separate myself and go pray somewhere. As it turns, that usually ended up being more my bedroom than the room I designated my prayer room/office at home. I think the things that surprised me the most is how He almost immediately changed my prayer time and included seeing the whole time. This *seeing* was different than the visions though.

The way I saw when praying was three different ways.

"The Well"

The Well, is what I call the first way He showed me. When it was the Well, it was as if I were down in a hole looking up. The mouth of the hole was wide, but I didn't seem to move toward the walls or try to climb out. I did not see my own body but would see as if looking up out of my eyes. In the first days of seeing this way, the Lion of Judah came to the well and looked in at me. Remembering correctly, it was as if He were upright, wearing clothes.

I then saw others come that I would later know are Host of Heaven. They came to the edge and also looked down into the well at me. He was not explaining at first, but then again, I was not asking. Perhaps that's what they all were waiting for.

Finally, one day I did ask. After all, I was starting to feel like I'd done something wrong. What was this? He was quick to answer, but He did not tell me. He showed me. I was in the hole looking up, and I saw a friend come to the rim of the hole. Even though everything I saw from the hole was in sort-of muted shiny tones, of light and dark, I could see her with her crazy waves and curls, her face, just her, clearly. She was peering down and looked very distraught. I saw her and I recognized she was distraught. Then I started asking God why and praying for her. As I did, just as I said before, I just knew. Again, I just knew. He made me know that moment what the Well was for! The Well was for interceding for people I knew. He was going to bring them there for me to see, and I was supposed to pray for them. I was amazed!

After that, he brought many I know, and I interceded for them.

"The Hard Place"

The next way I was shown, was what I call The Hard Place". It looked like two mountain ranges, but was always shown in almost completely dark, like night. There would just be enough light to make out the surroundings. Though I could not feel anything, it still somehow felt cold. My gaze would always be from a bit of a distance, but always highlighting the dry, rocky part between the two ranges.

In this place, I saw people all the time. They would go by one by one, coupled, or several at a time. It was always changing, always interesting. Just as the Well, I just watched this for several times really, before I even asked what it was about. I would look intently because it seemed there were many different periods of clothing. Long after seeing them, I would wonder what it all meant. The other interesting thing about this place is that at one point, a person, and then another time a couple, got close to a large rock in my view, and when they happened to look my way, they saw me! They looked shocked. I felt shocked! I didn't know what to do, so I waved. I did start asking the Lord what this was about. He told me that many, throughout the ages, were faced with making hard decisions. This came with a struggle. He said that this was like a valley of decision when people did not know what to do. I thought for a time that this must be just showing me the hardships people carried throughout the ages, because of the variety of clothing, but that was not the only thing. Near the end of seeing the Hard Place, I saw a young, very anointed woman that I knew from church, peeking around a rock there, with her head covered. From talking to her later, I believe this is something she does when she prays. So, it seemed it encompassed our time as well.

"The Holy Place"

The third way I would see when I started to pray didn't happen every time, but when it did, I could hardly breathe. I called this the Holy Place. It, like the Hard Place seemed set between two mountain ranges. The surroundings were also dark or maybe darkened so I could take it. This place was filled with angels!

In a way they seemed to move often in unison, and beautifully. There was such awe that rose within me, that it sometimes felt like my heart stopped or something. A few times I cried. The thing that was different about the Holy Place compared to the others is, I could not speak. There was no asking questions or continuing to pray. The only time that deviated from that was one morning. I saw it but saw no one. A song rose within me and I started to sing, still watching. Out of the caves and from behind the rocks came hundreds of angels. They lined up in rows on two sides. My heart was elated! Everything inside of me thought I was about to hear the angels sing! They didn't. Instead, they held their arms up and started swaying to the song I was singing. They were praising the Lord with me! It was beautiful, mesmerizing to see.

Even now I cannot adequately describe what the spirit within me felt that morning. This period reminds me greatly of Jeremiah 33:3: *"Call to me, and I will answer you, and show you great and mighty things, which you do not know." NKJV*

CHAPTER THREE

The Gift Called Forth

Time was passing. I was still seeing things and still experiencing the Well, the Hard Place, and the Holy Place. He also seemed to be adding back some regular prayer time, and integrating the normal way He and I operated for years before.

I am conversational with the Lord all day, not just at times. Sometimes I miss asking about a decision or something, but generally, it had been normal for me to make Him part of everything, whether good, bad, or indifferent, even before that vacation.

I knew there was a purpose for it all being stepped up though, but I didn't know what that purpose was. A mix of frustration and what felt like anxiety seemed to be rising within me. I knew we aren't supposed to fear. After all, Philippians 4:6-7 (NKJV) says: *"6 Be anxious for nothing, but in everything by prayer and supplication, with thanksgiving, let your requests be made known to God; 7 and the peace of God, which surpasses all understanding, will guard your hearts and minds through Christ Jesus."* So, I did know not to allow the uncertainty to cause me anxiety.

I think maybe I had entertained so many possible reasons, I just wanted to know for sure.

So, I stormed God's ears. It got to the point for at least two weeks that the only thing I asked is "What am I supposed to do?" and "You gave me this for a reason, I don't want to not do whatever it is I am supposed to do!" I would get so boisterous I would end up having to ask forgiveness and repent over it all, again. Still, there was nothing but the crickets chirping, and my heart sinking in the silence.

Then one day, a beautiful Saturday in August, I went into my room to pray. I got on the bed and just started talking to God. A little while later I did end up praying and asking the Lord to please let me know what He wanted from me. I also asked Him why He gave me a seer gift at all if I wasn't supposed to do anything with it! Then I listened and looked. Only silence, not a cricket chirp, not traffic, not a dog bark, nothing did I hear. So, I swallowed the lump in my throat, and laying there a thought came through my mind about things being in His time.

Ha ha, this part makes me laugh at the memory! I told the Lord right then that it was "okay" because I knew it was His timing, not mine. Oh my, I wish I could've seen His face right then because later it occurred to me that it was Him that reminded me not the other way around! Oops!

Thank goodness He is a good, good God, and He knows our reactions before we have them. He was very gracious and never said a word. Still, I recognized aloud my mistake and I asked Him to forgive me, and then laughed a little at myself.

I decided that I ought to let that go and get busy with something else. I had a project waiting out on the carport side of my husband's building. So, I said, "Lord, I'm not going to ask you anything about that again. I just want to ask You for a scripture or a passage or something today. Not for that, just for today, Lord." Then, well, no answer, again. So, I thought I'd just go on with the day, and I swung my legs around. I jumped off the bed, and the second my feet hit the floor, in my right ear I heard, "Isaiah 6:9."

Oh my gosh, it was awesome! It also instantly stopped me in my tracks! I heard it, audibly. I'd only heard something audibly, like a person was standing right there, once before. That was years earlier during a very tragic and dangerous moment.

I turned around to look for my bible, but it wasn't there. I remembered it was in the living room and I ran in there and grabbed it. I feverishly looked for Isaiah but in the rush and excitement, to my surprise, I couldn't seem to find it, even with the tabs. Finally, I found it, yes! I didn't look at verse 9. I decided to just read Isaiah 6 period, then I could keep it in context. I know a lot of scripture, but I don't necessarily always know where it's at. This was one of those times.

In fact, during 6 ½ years of doing praise and worship, I used to sing a song based on it! Then, I got to verse 9: *"And He said, "Go and tell this people: Keep on hearing, but do not understand; Keep on seeing, but do not perceive."* NKJV. Wow!

Then it was like He was prompting me internally to read it again, so I started at the top again. Before I got to 9, I had started quivering in my body and voice noticeably. Just as I got right at 9, He highlighted what was above it in that bible, "Isaiah's Commissioning to be Prophet". My eyes read it but for a second or two it did not sink in. So, as I was finishing 9 and going on to 10, then it hit me. Right then, this kid at Christmas excitement was just all inside me, and I got His intention. Out loud I was saying something like, "Oh my gosh, Lord! This is where You commissioned Isaiah to be a Prophet, and You used the same words to me, and now You're commissioning me?!" Honestly, I did say it almost as a question. Then He brought back an encounter and vision I had over 6 years beforehand.

The Writing in Stone

I was leaving for work, and just as I was walking around the end of the couch to go to the door, the room around me kind-of blued-out. What I mean by that, is a muted tone of Robin's egg blue seemed to be around me. This is nothing like my home is!

The room as I knew it, the door, the furniture, etc., all gone. I stopped abruptly and was trying to grasp what was going on. Then I realized there was a light coming from somewhere above me. I looked up but I could not see the source. Just as I got done looking up at the light, this thing came down with a boom. It had fallen right before my feet! When I looked down, it appeared as a bumpy rock formation. Then I was made to look closer and I saw the words:

END TIMES PROPHET

In caps, and big enough I wondered how I could have missed the words the first time. Then I just stood there, trying to wrap my head around what was happening, and then replaying the words of the rock in my head. Then I just knew what was happening! He was telling me that in the end times, I would be a Prophet, for Him!

The very second, I figured that out, a bouquet of long-stemmed red roses fell from above on top of the stone. I felt that Christmas inside me excitement and a huge elation moving over me, like when you receive a gift. Then I realized, I did just receive a gift, or I would at some point. It just wasn't for now. I was so excited! Then I felt a hand on the right side of my upper chest and shoulder. It was almost like when someone holds an arm out and puts a hand against you to stop you from jetting forward on a quick stop. I knew it was an angel, but the moment I felt it, inside it was like a reminder, "Remember, not now, the end times." So, I agreed, and I never forgot. I just have had many experiences, so I kind-of filed it away somewhere inside, knowing it wasn't for then.

That day I knew standing there, having read Isaiah 6, being given Isaiah 6:9, and being reminded of the encounter all those years before, that *this was it*. What was foretold back then was now coming to fruition. I was overwhelmed, excited, then I re-read it again, and right about verse 10, the fear of the Lord rose within me!

I knew He anointed me for this task but was it that task, the same specifics of Isaiah? I guessed it was. Better than me trying to explain why, I will give you the passage entirely, that you might see why the excitement was quickly followed by almost a heaviness. The heaviness, I know was because of the fear of the Lord, which is good, rose in me. The fear of the Lord in me recognized the Lord's sovereignty and the gravity of it was the responsibility that came with the gift. Therefore, Isaiah 6:

"1 In the year that King Uzziah died, I saw the Lord sitting on the throne, high and lifted up, and the train of His robe filled the temple,

Above it stood seraphim; each with six wings: with two he covered his face, with two he covered his feet, and with two he flew,

And one cried to another and said: "Holy, holy holy is the Lord of hosts; The whole earth is full of His glory!"

And the posts of the door were shaken by the voice of Him who cried out, and the house was filled with smoke,

So I said, "Woe is me, for I am undone!

Because I am a man of unclean lips, and I dwell in the midst of a people with unclean lips; For my eyes have seen the King, the Lord of hosts.

Then one of the seraphim flew to me, having in his hand a live coal which he had taken with the tongs from the altar.

And he touched my lips with it and said: "Behold this has touched your lips; Your iniquity is taken away, and your sin purged."

Also I heard the voice of the Lord, saying: "Whom shall I send, and And who will go for Us?" Then I said, "Here I am! Send me."

And he said, "Go and tell this people: 'Keep on hearing, but do not understand; Keep on seeing, but do not perceive.'

"Make the heart of this people dull, And their ears heavy, And shut their eyes; Lest they see with their eyes, And hear with their ears, And understand with their heart, And return and be healed.

Then I said, "Lord, how long?" And He answered: "Until the cities are laid waste and without inhabitant, The houses are without a man, The land is utterly desolate,

The Lord has removed men far away, And the forsaken places are many in the midst of the land.

But yet a tenth will be in it, And will return and be for consuming, As a terebinth tree or as an oak, Whose stump remains when it is cut down. So, the holy seed shall be its stump.

   Isaiah 6:1-13 NKJV.

   So, that day in August I was now sure of two things. One, my life wasn't going to be the same, and we must be now be walking in the "end times".

CHAPTER FOUR

Glimpses of What It Is Like

L ooking back, a lot has happened in a short amount of time. Sometimes it is difficult to remember it all. It doesn't help that I have been horrible at journaling it consistently. I would write on the closest thing to me, sticky notes, notebook paper, the back of bill envelopes, whatever was near. I bought several journal books, a certain kind, and every once and awhile would write things in them, but normally all my notes and good intentions got lost or misplaced, and generally were in multiple places all at once. For this I have asked the Lord to forgive me, and I send my apologies to you as well.

In the process of writing this, I was reminded of things that have happened. They were within this period, so I will outline them now.

They Know You Can See Now

During the Well, Hard Place, and the Holy Place, there was one night, where all of a sudden about five to six men appeared. They weren't really men, they were demons, but appeared as men dressed in casual clothes. I was stunned. I lay there silent, still with eyes shut, and just watched. They were shaking fists at me. They looked like they were yelling, but I could not hear them. One particularly seemed so livid!

I'm not sure how I knew or thought of it at that moment, but I said, "No. You can't be here. You must leave! Go, in the name of Jesus!" Then they turned to their left, and started walking away. The one that seemed livid, lagged, and the one that had been beside him reached back and grabbed him by the shirt he was wearing. It was so strange! Afterward the thought that ran through my head was, "They know you can see now." That moment I assumed it was my thought. Over time, I realized it was likely a ministering angel.

Hosts & Wings & Special Things

From the time I got home, it was evident that life had changed. What I didn't mention so far, is the fact that I wasn't seeing nearly as many visions like the plane, as I was just "seeing" pretty much all the time. I started seeing the heavenly host everywhere. Very quickly, I came to think that most people wouldn't do half of what they do now if they knew the large company that is around us all the time! I meant it, and I still think so!

Did you know that usually angels don't show their wings? In fact, I would go out on a limb and say it's been my experience that usually they don't.

It started slowly, then as time went on, more often, I would catch a glimpse, or open my eyes to see them. One of the most surprising ways was the first couple times I saw them materialize, in the daytime, in a room with more than just me! It was like something you'd see in a movie and I just remember being blown away; part of me wishing my husband could see them too, and part of me feeling like I was experiencing and sitting on this huge secret! When they materialized, they would be fully seen but also fully seen through. The outline of their wardrobe seemed almost like crystal or sparkly diamond edges, and somehow, I could see details like piping or what seemed like embroidery or beards, etc. even though I could clearly see through them too. The moment I saw it I was awed.

The second moment I remembered I'd seen it before, probably about thirteen years before. That time, it was just one. After reading Luke and praying for a long time and then falling asleep, I awoke with a start. When I hopped off my bed, I went to the door that was at my dining room at that time. He was tall, very tall. He wore an odd-looking, tall hat. He was all outlines also. Still I saw that he was wearing robes and there was a sort-of vine with leaves that seemed part of the edging. He did not look my way, but I remember I was fixated, but did not move or speak as he glided past me and just made it under the wood-work leading to the kitchen.

It is awesome. It truly is. However, we do not worship angels. Angels were created by God, just like we were. If they minister to us or "save" us in an accident or any of those things people sometimes think, it is because it is their job. Another part some-times folks do not understand, when we pass, we do not become angels. We are us, and they are them. They were not people that have passed on, and we do not morph into angels when we get to heaven. In saying this, I mean no offense to people that have believed that way. Sometimes many have been comforted with the thoughts because they have lost a young child or a brother or sister. No one that has Jesus who passes is disappointed that they are not angels, because they are God's children, and what they gain there is worth far more than a pair of wings! I do real-ize that what I have been given is awesome, and not a gift every-one seems to get. I do appreciate it. Still, I think He gives us what is needful or useful for what He will have us do here. It's not be-cause I am so great, because believe me, I am not. He is, and He has a purpose and a plan for everything He does.

"10 As each one has received a gift, minister to one another, as good stewards of the manifold grace of God." I Peter 4:10 NKJV

As amazing a gift it is, at times, it has been overwhelming. When you go from having mostly dreams and every now and again a vision, to seeing all the time and things seeming to be added, it can really make everything seem like too much to process. Early on I experienced going from excited to just worn out, depleted. Adding to that, if the enemy comes to mess with you, it can very quickly get you out of faith or faltering or falling.

It wasn't just the heavenly host I now was seeing. Yeah, . . . the other side.

Demons Really Exist

I wasn't going to capitalize that title. I make a point not to glorify what the enemy (devil, demons, witchcraft, etc.) has done, because if I am doing that, then I am not glorifying God. Additionally, when we have Holy Spirit *in* us, the power of God can work *through* us. I'm sure you know, but if you don't, God trumps the devil. Does that mean we should tempt or taunt the dark side? I would advise against it. Sometimes though, even if you are not actively dealing with a sin issue, which leaves a door open, you can still experience the enemy. In fact, if you are trying to do anything for God, trying to be led, trying to be faithful, you will become a target at some point! Two scriptures come to mind:

"8 Be sober, be vigilant; because your adversary the devil walks about like a roaring lion, seeking whom he may devour." I Peter 5:8 NKJV, and *"11Put on the whole armor of God, that you may be able to stand against the wiles of the devil."* Ephesians 6:11 NKJV

A Horde from Hell

One late Saturday morning I was alone in the house with the dogs and the heavenly entourage. I wasn't necessarily seeing them, by then I just knew they are always there. I decided to take some time to pray and praise. I turned on YouTube and one of the groups I like to listen to. I was singing and intermittently praying.

Then praising turned into serious prayer. It seemed to have changed to fervent and only in tongues now. I knew I must be talking with God about something serious. I didn't have a staff, per se, at that time. So, I went and grabbed this wooden rod or dowel out of a crock we use like an umbrella stand. I was marching around and holding that up, like Moses, leading the

Children of Israel with it, ha ha!

Suddenly I saw this horde of people running full bore toward me from the east. It didn't even dawn on me at the time that I was seeing outside, a field where there is none, and inside the room I was in, all at once. They ran right through where the wall and windows are. It sounds cliché to say that they were all wearing black, but I can't help what it sounds like, they were! They all appeared as male, wearing various clothing. Some were gnashing teeth and some looked as that one before, like they were yelling, but I could not hear, only see. Again, I am not sure where I got the where-with-all, because I will tell you that I was startled and felt a little frozen when they came barreling in. It was shocking, and not in a good way. However, Holy Spirit must have led because I did much as before, I just opened my mouth and said something like, "No. Get out! You cannot be here, so go! In the name of Jesus!" Then, to my surprise, without any of the fanfare they arrived with, they simply turned and walked away. I could not believe it. I could not believe it! After thanking God that he helped me through it, I called my best friend to tell her what I just saw. She's seen a lot and experienced a lot too. In her normal fashion, she just said, "Well, that's weird." Yep, it was. I will relay one more here that was "just weird."

Over time I had seen both heavenly and evil things. However, I have also seen what I can only describe as people in different period clothing, and then one that seemed like a person that looked dead. I have never watched all the zombie series' that were out, nor did I want to. However, one weekend, looking out our French doors and looking sort-of northwest, I saw what appeared to be a gray, dead-looking man with a hat standing in the nearby field. He was still but looking at me. I'm not sure why I got so angry, but I remember saying serious and out loud, "Oh no you don't!" See, I thought I'd seen this one before, and many others across the field to the north. They seemed to be moving around and having a good time along the tree-line near the vacant house there. I wasn't sure what might've happened there but after seeing things moving around over there, I got my husband's binoculars. It seemed like I was seeing something from some past time. It appeared that maybe someone had a bar or a brothel out here in the middle of nowhere. It looked like men and women dressed and undressed around the grounds and in trees. The one now in my field I saw leaning on a tree, standing there alone. I know it seems far-fetched, and I know that it does not necessarily fit the way demons usually show themselves, but it is what happened.

There it was. So, I went about pointing at it through my door and telling it very loudly, then yelling, that it could not come on the property, that it had to turn around and go back where it came from! I knew what to do, and I was serious! I thought I'd said, "In the name of Jesus," but now I'm not sure. Either way, I walked away believing it was taken care of. To be honest, I was prideful. I didn't even stay at the door to see if it left! So, imagine my surprise when I went glanced out a bit later saw it still in the field, but much closer! This time, though, I got my act together. I told it again that it could not come onto the property, I *loosed it* from me, *bound it,* and told it to go back where it came from, *in the name of Jesus*! This time it left. Later, I saw where I sent it. It was back at the tree, but it seemed stuck there. I didn't know any better at the time, so I left it like that until much later when I just cleared that whole area out.

Why do I tell you this, when to this day I am not sure exactly what it was? I guess because there are things here in this life on earth that will never make sense until we meet Him one day, and then it, thankfully, will no longer matter.

He is God and we are not. People say that God will never give you more than you can handle, but nothing in the Bible says that. What it does say, however, is when we are weak, He is strong. Whether weary from the battle, angry or allowing fear in, I have learned to run to God, not away. Even like this, when I just don't have a grid for something, I don't try to make sense of it or figure it out first. I run to Him first.

CHAPTER FIVE

The Court of Heaven-My Experience

Before any folks that happen to believe says, "Hey, you're just getting that from Robert Henderson!" No, that's not true. I would suggest that people read, listen and watch Robert Henderson about the Courts of Heaven. He has a lot more detail. The truth of the matter is, I only have my own experience with it, being taken into a court of heaven, unexpectedly in the fall of 2016. My encounter happened every night I went to bed for about seven weeks. Plus, I never heard of Robert Henderson or the "Courts of Heaven," until my experience had been over for a while. Then when visiting an old friend I used to intercede with, I shared my experience. She got very excited and ask if I had heard about Robert Henderson. When I told her no, she pulled out CDs she had of his experience and all he'd learned. I took them home and was blown away. In fact, I'm not sure I ever got those CDs back to her. Sorry, Diane!

I went to bed one night. My husband was not in the room, or not in the room yet. As I rounded the far corner of my side of the bed, I saw white. I turned and saw even more white, both hanging and moving in the room. It seemed almost cloud-like, but just a connected patch, lingering. As I turned and got into bed, I looked again. There was more, and it seemed to be coming into the room from the same door I just walked through. By now I had already seen so much, it didn't shock me as much as I just thought, "Well, this is new." I got into bed and looked up and I saw people looking back at me. They seemed to be sitting or taking seats in what looked like theater seats. I say that because the chairs seemed like the flip-down ones I would sit in to go watch a movie or a play. They came down the same way so that folks in the back could see as well as the ones up front.

It was no longer a patch of lingering white. I saw people. The clothing or robes seemed generally similar, yet not the same. They were shown in white and their attire had black or dark gray detail, but I feel that maybe that was just so I could see detail. In a way, most that I saw looked like from another time, or in attire for this occasion whatever it was. I still can see them in my mind's eye. So that night, and for several nights, I just laid there. I said my prayers. I looked at them. They looked at me. I don't think it was until days in that I even made any statements to them, rather just commented to the Lord. Finally, though, I did say something like, "Boy, you guys must be really bored. I can't believe you are here and just watch me sleep." I am probably paraphrasing here, but it was close. Three to four weeks went by this way. It became so common for me, I would wish them a good night and such. Somewhere in there, I began to wonder if these were my "cloud of witnesses."

Then a night came that changed the whole dynamic! A tall man came in. When he entered, the whole atmosphere changed. Even the ones sitting in the stands seemed to feel the difference. Me, laying on my bed, I felt the difference! My view was still clear but somehow still seemed darker.

I looked very closely at him. He seemed very serious. His clothes seemed from another time, but very proper. He wore a long fitted-type coat, that had designer-type fitting and detail, and he wore a hat. I feel like I will remember that hat for the rest of my life here on earth!

It was black. It reminded me of a western hat, but it was low on top with a large rim. I am not sure why the hat stood out so much, but it did. As it was large, the rim that is, I felt like I never clearly saw his face, except twice. I did twice. He had a pencil-type mustache, that reminds me of the villains in old-time movies or cartoons. The first time I saw him clearly, was when he turned to point in my direction. It was what I would call a dead-eye stare. It sent shivers through me! Though he had already been there almost two weeks at that point, I feel I was naïve. Until that moment it was merely just a passing thought of who he might be. That moment, however, I was sure. He was the devil! Then I realized he was also the prosecuting attorney, and I was the defendant simply laying on my bed. Oh my gosh, this wasn't theater! This was a court; and I was on trial! Ugh, it was so unsettling and hard to conceive!

Now the atmosphere was even darker. Every night I dreaded going back in my room, knowing I was entering the court again. I would try not to look at all, or look only at the original people in the stands. I'd shut my eyes, but it would do no good. Since I see in the spirit, I would still see the proceedings. Sometimes I would be present for a long time. Sometimes I would be tired enough or blessed enough, to fall asleep.

I have never asked but I wonder now if I could only see and not hear because God knew it was more than my heart or mind could bear. I wonder now if the grace of God extended through the process so I didn't just lose it altogether.

I will say this, even not hearing him, I know he is ruthless! From the moment he entered the courts, he never left. My entire life and anything I did, large or small, must have been presented, and with great fervency. I could have been my bed pillow. There was nothing I could do. A few times I called out to God or the spectators, "What is going on?" I received no answers. The faces of the crowd in the stands though, seemed a mix of downtrodden or trying not to show any emotion at all. My feelings sank even more because up until him, it felt like I had a company of friends. I suppose I just eventually realized that this is what was happening. I had to realize whatever was happening would happen through completion. After that, there were occasional moments that felt like some terrible turn just happened, or things felt like it was not looking good for me overall. Then, one night

I simply said something like, "I have no excuses or justifications, but one. I plead the Blood of Christ! I plead the Blood of Christ!"

My speaking or pleading seemed to disrupt everything for a few moments.

The spectators were all looking at me, and the devil turned, and he looked so angry! That was the second time I saw his face. I realized right then that yes, these proceedings would go on, but I learned something. I learned that when I felt that heaviness come, like it was all over for me, that I could plead the blood. So, I did. I didn't lay there and do it all the time. I did it when I felt hope was fleeting. Each time, I did it until I felt a release and just let them do whatever they were doing.

Then, at the end of the 7th week, these doors at the end of this grand hall we were all either in, or party to, came open. Coming toward all of us another tall man appeared.

The atmosphere was tense. It felt like high static in the air. It was a tenseness but not with the same heaviness. There was both awe and fear. I can honestly say that I could not look to see what the crowd looked like because I was fixated on the one that entered.

He came quickly and walking as if he were serious about something. As he came closer, I knew who it was. I had seen him before. It was Jesus! Yes, Jesus was in the courtroom! My heart was in my throat. I doubt I took a breath at all.

He was wearing a long and brilliantly white robe. He had a sash, which would be about where the bottom of His belly would be. I think he must've had sandals on, or he was barefoot, because I have some remembrance of seeing His toes.

He walked right up to the devil and stood chest to chest with him. The look on His face was intense, and the look in His eyes was either an intense seriousness or anger. This might seem like a dramatic build-up with a seemingly simple ending. I do not think I have not forgotten. I am not withholding. I saw no words exchanged. I saw them chest to chest and the look on Jesus's face. Then, that was it.

Suddenly it was as if everything ended. Everyone got up and started moving. The court must've been dismissed. I don't even remember watching Jesus or the devil leaving! I think I just panicked and thought, "Oh no!" and started asking, "What happened? Have I been found guilty? Where is everyone going?" Then I looked toward the stands and they were nearly empty. Only the last ones were milling out to the aisle between the seats. I started crying like my heart was weeping. Right about then, a man, woman, and a child who had been in the stands came. They stood before me and they smiled and waved. I was stunned! I realized I was smiling back, and I waved. Then behind them, another, then more. It didn't go on long and it wasn't the whole crowd of them, but many. It was like they came to say good-bye, but their faces were friendly, even happy. Then, so was I.

I am not sure how I did not figure it out 'til that moment. Jesus came. All He had to do is come in! That's all it took to end the whole thing, Him, just Him.

As menacing as the devil was or seemed to be, he was no match for Jesus. Without a word, He set me free, again. Any remnant of sorrow or trepidation turned to glee.

Though I never saw him cast out, this verse comes to mind;

"Then I heard a loud voice saying in heaven, 'Now salvation, and strength, and the Kingdom of our God, and the power of the Christ has come, for the accuser of our brethren, who accused them before our God day and night, has been cast down.'" NKJV

Chapter SIX

A Journey is a Climb

To move forward with how I got to where I am now, we must move back. To remind you, when He dropped the stone in front of me that said, "End Times Prophet," He also made me know right then that it was not for then, but in the "end times." He had an angel touch me on my right upper shoulder and chest as if to, again remind me. It was that important! He often works this way, telling or showing you something but it not coming to fruition for years, sometimes decades. On that note, sometimes it never does. Instead, people may be shown things that will happen, but in a future time, that they will never see.

In the case of Moses, he never got to the promised land God told him of, rather he got to come close and see it, then die in the wilderness. He had sinned against God by hitting the rock instead of speaking to it, after getting implicit instructions. The story starts in Exodus 17:6 but doesn't end until Moses's death in Deuteronomy 34. There God lets him see it with his eyes, and reinforces it being given to the remaining children of Israel, but did not allow him to cross over.

Every person has their own journey with Him. Just as our fingerprints are different, so are all of us. Every person has needs, wants, has certain bends or tendencies. We all have strengths and weaknesses. We also all fall.

What do I mean by that? Well, we all sin. If that isn't something you know or think about, it is simply thinking things or doing things that are against Him, against God. I don't mean to offend. I don't take it as offense either. No one is perfect. Some might come much closer than me, but no one is perfect. Romans 3:23 says, "for all have sinned and fall short of the glory of God."

Meditating on Moses's story sure makes me glad that Jesus came to earth after that, and ultimately was the atonement, so that I, or you, could be reconciled with our Creator. In laymen's terms, He paid the price for every time we "hit the rocks" and went against God. He paid the price. I want to point out that it is past tense, meaning, He already did it. It's done. All we must do to partake of the gift given, is simply believe and accept it and Him. That's it. There's no magic pill, no long series of classes, no checklists to complete. There is nothing that we can add to what He did to save ourselves. He did all that needed done. All He did was leave it our decision. He loved us enough to save us, but gave us the choice to accept it or not and accept Him or not. I liken it to a relationship where one person truly loves another and is willing to give everything they have, to put that person ahead and above themselves.   That's great in theory, but as humans, we fail sometimes. So, though maybe some out there are those kinds of people and try to the best of their abilities, they still don't do it perfectly. Jesus did.

God could have made us mindless robots to follow obediently and without question, He didn't. I compare that part to marriage. Do we want our spouse to come to us, or stay with us out of love or out of obligation? In the bible, Genesis 1:27 says: *"So God created man in his own image; in the image of God he created him; male and female he created them."*

This means we are created to have traits of God. We are modeled after the Creator. He wanted us to choose a relationship with Him, not make us have one. Wouldn't you feel the same? I do.

Perhaps most folks have a quicker journey than I had to get to where I needed to be to start to fulfill my call, I'm not sure. I can only relay what the journey has been like for me. It has been slow-moving, like walking uphill with backpacks filled with rocks at times. Then again, I know that the journey here on earth never actually completes until it is our appointed time to move on to our eternal destiny.

The hiker with the backpacks filled with rocks is much as I was filled with burdens, anxiety, and sin. I was walking forward, but it was slow because I had to have things removed, or adjusted, and ultimately lay it all down at the feet of God. Each time He moved me enough that some of that baggage was cut off or laid down, all the world's yokes I entangled myself with started breaking, and His yoke started to encompass me more greatly.

To paint a picture, the cumbersome things were being left behind were like bags dropped on the hillside. He was moving me and helping me overcome. It was tough at first. It was hard to walk forward and move up to a better place. As a hiker builds muscle and momentum, so did I. With things starting and continuing to be cut away, I was not as weighed down and I could walk forward easier, and at a quicker pace.

The more I read the Word of God, prayed, or even just sought answers about belief, the more strength I seemed to have. I noticed my choices were changing. Hard things for me to kick, like cigarettes, eventually were overcome. It is a process that might slow down after a time, but if you are trying to walk with God, it is a process that just keeps working. No two journeys are alike. Everyone's journey begins when He creates us. Then, sometime later, we start getting glimpses or clues, just starting to pull us toward Him. These are seeds.

Who Is That?

We moved to a little village halfway through Kindergarten. Though I was shy back then, I made a few friends, local girls. At seven, one of them handed me a flyer for vacation bible school. I had no clue what that was. Even at seven, I was torn because part of me wanted to go; but the insecure girl with a lot of anxiety didn't want anything to do with the unknown! All these decades later I realize there is truly a battle of good and evil that fights for even the youngest kids! So, on the appointed days, I walked over the hill two or three houses away to the little local Presbyterian church where it was held.

I remember one of the times I got in a bit of trouble. Glancing around, I saw a picture of the crucifixion. Jesus was hanging there on a cross. It seemed dark and sad, and I was fixated on it. I was lost in it. Apparently, the teacher asked me a question and I never even heard her. I was just staring at that picture. She scolded me because I wasn't paying attention!

When the classes were over, the other girls I knew stopped going to the church. I couldn't believe it! After learning what Jesus did for all of us, I couldn't believe they would just stop going! So, I went by myself. I would sit with the whole congregation and listen. I can't say I remembered anything from there, but I believe God had gotten ahold of the heart within me.

After a while, it felt like something was missing, but I wasn't sure what. Discerning that, I walked myself over to the only other church in the village, the Methodist Church. The very first time I felt even more of something was missing there. Then I surmised that it wasn't fair to judge it by only going one time, so I would go twice more, just to make sure, and give it a fair chance. Two more weeks I walked to the Methodist Church, and two more weeks I felt it wasn't where I was supposed to be or something. So, after my trial period, I walked myself back over the Presbyterian church. Ha ha! I always giggle a little bit when I remember that.

Snuffing Out the Gift

For about three to four years, ending in my 13th year, the supernatural presented itself in my life in a bigger way than it had ever been present before. I sporadically had bad dreams even younger; this was different though. This was every night, and would now be called "night terrors." God didn't cause this. The night terrors were likely able to come because a door was opened, caused by some great trauma. With trauma, doors also, unfortunately, open to the devil and his minion demons. This is the first place in my life I am sure that my eyes were opened to the supernatural realm. Prior to that, I am not sure if my eyes were open, or I just had a really elaborate imagination!

Every night I was woken up to see a thing or things staring back at me. The pinnacle of this happened in the 7th grade. As I said, I was thirteen. It had already gotten a little weird in the daytime, seeing what looked like a German Shepherd dog walking through the house, but up toward the ceiling. I had heard lots of noises, seen some faces in the windows when outside, just stuff.

One night, running around playing hide-n-seek and other games outside with the neighborhood kids, we all heard a huge crash from upstairs inside the house. It sounded like someone had pushed a full dresser over onto the floor or something! The parents were off working in my uncle's little grocery. It stopped all of us. Then my brother who didn't live there but was staying there at the time, was brave and took a bat or stick or something and told me to "Stay here." Man, I was so scared for him! After going in though, he found nothing out of place and absolutely nothing knocked over. As kids do, we all just went on, and just thought, "Huh?"

So, for that time, night after night I would wake up. Sometimes, I would wake and be laying in my own urine. I would be harassed and terrified by awful-looking things that would stand just a little from my bed, or others that would come close and look me dead in the eyes. I would just try to stay perfectly still and not make a sound. All the while, I would lay there trying to muster up enough courage to get out of my bed and run out of the room. Sometimes I did, many times, I did not. The times I made it, I usually jumped off the end of the bed and locked myself in the bathroom across the hall. The weird thing about it all, it occurred to me several years later that never once did I go to school that year and tell a friend, or my parents. The only thing I think is that maybe somewhere deep inside I wondered if I was going crazy, and I just could not bear to have them think it too.

Light Entered

Toward the end of the tortuous, harassing time, and without introduction, something changed. One night anticipating the worst, instead I just saw two small lights. They seemed orb-like, oval, and seemed to be about three feet off the ground. At first, I did what anyone would. I tried to see what was making the odd reflection that seemed to be hanging in mid-air, yet did seem to move ever so slightly. I couldn't find anything. Then I just watched them until I fell asleep. This became the new normal. It was still a little strange, but I could rest, thankfully.

We moved, and those lights seem to have followed me into the next house and the next year and a half of school. They did not seem to just be out in the open anymore though. More, I would catch a glimpse and then they would disappear. It was more like it was just enough that I knew they were there. At the time I didn't have a grid for this. I wondered if they were passed-on relatives or some other spirits? If so, I thought, they must have been good ones, because when I saw them, it would always be quiet and tranquil, even if the remainder of the day was not. With them, I was not afraid. I had peace.

I came to believe, and still do, that these were angels just taking another form. God already knew I would be His. I think satan either wanted to stop that or test that theory.

Like Job, I think he wanted to test me because he didn't want me to ever come to God. Plus, he's satan, he hates everyone, including his followers. Like Job, I think God allowed it, but said, "But you can only go this far." So, I believe when satan had reached his cut-off point, the Lord sent two angels to come and guard me.

And Then Came Him

When I was fifteen, I had become acquainted with a church my mom sometimes went to, 25-30 miles from where we lived. I had, at that time, an aunt, and a few cousins there. I don't remember what the circumstances were, if it was just regular church or if they were having a special guest. We were just there.

I do know that I was listening intently. I wasn't feeling like, "Uh, why do I have to be here?" I was interested. I wanted to see what it all was about.

The pastor described some things and he basically gave an alter call if anyone needed prayer, healing, or didn't know Jesus. My belly felt like it was being pulled up. I was scared to go and scared not to go. I was still shy in front of crowds then. I really wasn't trying to run from a move of God, or from God, Himself.

I can't remember if anyone went first. I just remember when I went, it seemed like just the pastor looking at me, and me. He asked what I needed. I think I told Him I wanted to accept Jesus. In my mind's ear, I vaguely recall some happy sounds coming from the congregation. The next moment though, it seemed all of them melted away.

He kind-of summarized what it meant, ask if I understood. I don't remember what else He said, but He had me repeat after him. I did. Then, as if my entire body had a mind of its own, I began shaking, and my mouth opened, and words were leaving my mouth I had never heard. It wasn't even English! I might have panicked, but I couldn't. It was a long trail that, seemed like it went on forever! I could tell people were elated.

I remember him announcing that I'd received the Holy Spirit too. I had witnessed others that spoke like this, but never knew much about that point at the time. I know. It seems weird. Sometimes, even Christians don't believe in an infilling of the Holy Spirit. Others think it was for only before. I have nothing against anyone that believes either way. I just know it is real. I also know that I still have that language. I believe it is my prayer language. It is the dominant language that comes out other than me talking in English. Long after that time, other languages emerged. I would estimate I speak at least four others for sure.

I figure that God had to give me the gift of tongues right then, because I was fifteen, and the enemy had already come for me several times in my life up to that point. At some point maybe I can tell you about that as well. It will likely be another book though.

Having a prayer language is a way that I can talk to God one on one, that leaves me, and my thoughts and my desires out of it. It also is something the devil cannot understand. So, when I speak in tongues, even now, it is talking to God and speaking back to Him His perfect will for whatever He and I are talking about.

That day I met the one that I had learned about a little, had felt offended for when my friends left that little church, the one who had protected me, and moved in and around me until that evening when I accepted Him. I felt different. I felt as if I could float away. That day I learned that there'd likely not been anything missing those eight years earlier at either of those churches! The thing I could feel inside that was missing, was the God-shaped hole that was filled completely that evening when I met Jesus.

He made Himself real to me. I was His. I will forever be grateful for that day. Though later I would start a trail of intermittently straying away and coming back, that day I was all His. Maybe the best part of all, He found me. He wooed me. He let little seeds be planted to ignite my curiosity, and He drew me. I will forever be grateful for that. "We love Him because he first loved us." I John 4:19

CHAPTER SEVEN

Working with God

I f you ask any pastor anywhere in the world, "What all has God had you do over time?" inevitably they will probably tell you, "Everything." Every man or woman I have ever met or known that is truly journeying with God, usually has a steady stream of things they've been told or felt led to do, which can be both regular grunt work and delving into the supernatural. Whether standing on a street corner being laughed at for trying to reach people that don't know Christ, scrubbing the toilets of the local church assembly, or manning a food kitchen to feed the hungry, God doesn't lead his to shy away from seemingly menial tasks. In fact, He will send you right to them. My journey has been no different.

GOD DREAMS
As an adult, both in and out of church, I started having dreams again. These were not night terrors, even though some had elements that I did not like or that seemed negative. I don't even know how to explain to you how I knew these were from God, I just did. To repeat a phrase, I feel I have found myself saying a lot in life, "I just know."

These dreams went on through several long patches. They would come for a period and then go, just to come back some other time. Sometimes I was completely perplexed and sometimes they made me think of something and I would pray about it. All the while I was sure they meant something, and God wanted me to know that something. They became spiritual puzzles. I tried to figure them out. I went through times of writing them down, and then other times of just being lazy or forgetful with it. After all, there had been so many!

At some point, I had my heart broken severely. I was pacing and crying and beseeching God, wanting Him to change the situation. In the middle of all that, I cried out, "Lord you show me all these things, but I don't know what I am supposed to do! I don't know what much of it even means! Please! Can't You just interpret the important parts for me?" Then, as if that's all He was waiting on, He did. In my mind's eye he replayed just a bit of what I had seen at that time, and I "just knew" what most of it meant. From that time on, when I have a God dream, I seem to easily know what almost all of it means. Still, He seems to hold one thing back every time, ha ha. I think He likes leaving me one golden nugget so I must keep pressing in and searching for the answer. I think I love that about Him!

Getting Hands On

Some of the most crucial and memorable times I have ever had is when God had cut enough self-focus or selfishness out of me to get me involved in a church that was based on Him and helping others. I was blessed to be welcomed into an awesome group of people who really lived out their belief!

During that time, I cooked dishes and served at Saturday luncheons. I learned a lot then. It was set up for the needy. To my surprise, it wasn't always the needy that came! In fact, I would say most of the folks that came had enough to buy their own food, etc. Still, what God seemed to explain to me when I questioned that part, is that while they all didn't need the food, they did all need something. They needed someone that cared, they needed Him.

The pastor of this church felt led to start a homeless shelter. It was around that same time, God told me He was going to lead me to do something else, minister.

To be honest, elements of my life had been so hard; I just

didn't want one more thing. He's sure got a way though! The parking lot where I worked was also the parking lot for the church. Everyday people from the shelter were standing against the wall that bordered the bus station. Every day I would have to go out to get in my car. Conversations started taking place. Through church and those encounters, I got to know them all, sometimes helped with this or that.

A whole year later, God tapped me on the shoulder and asked me if I knew what I'd been doing. Then he reminded me of the day he told me I would minister. Then He connected the last year and the friends I had made, and the conversations I had and the thoughts I relayed. I was blown away, like it was a big surprise! What I thought of with "minister" wasn't what He thought. Again, it was like they needed Him. So, He told my pastor to create a shelter and he sent a bunch of people, including me, to care for them, and show them Him. It has always felt that I came away from there with way more blessings than maybe they received. That is true except for those that left and had Him.

During and after that time I got to go two counties away every Saturday for six years, and every other Saturday for one year, and pick up carloads, truckloads, and trailer loads of bread. I would then take them back to my county and distribute to 7 churches and a couple individuals. They would then give them away to the hungry. I met a whole network of people moving behind the scenes in big ways for God. It was awesome, some of my best memories! *"For I was hungry and you gave me food; I was thirsty and you gave Me drink; I was naked and you clothed Me; I was in prison and you came to Me. The righteous will answer Him, saying 'Lord, when did we see You hungry and feed You, or thirsty and give You drink? Or when did we see You sick, or in prison, and come to You? And the King will answer and say to them, 'Assuredly, I say to you, inasmuch as you did it to one of the least of these My brethren, you did it to Me'."* Matthew 25: 35-40 NKJV

Intercession

For anyone that does not know the term, intercession simply means to intercede for something. In this case, it is praying, but it is at a different level than just speaking words.

Usually when a person is called to intercession, an anointing for it from God accompanies. A tell-tale sign of someone that is an Intercessor is when they are burdened heavily by others' plights, or by certain things God brings to their attention. It is more than passing interest, or say a prayer and then go on. It usually leaves one in intercession pacing, sweating, up at nights, crying, contending, like a prize fighter, because *they are* in the spiritual realm.

Prior to helping hands on in a church, He had already moved me into intercession. For periods of time before and after, it seemed to have become my "main thing," so to speak. It wasn't that He took things from me, like the God dreams. More, it was as if He was adding to. I have had the privilege over time to take many people and issues, both that I knew and did not know, both local and nationally or world-wide to God. To be honest, it was not really easy, ever. It also was and is exhausting. If you know bible, then you know the "Woman with the Issue of Blood" story. She had suffered long with a debilitating issue. She knew Jesus was the only one that could help her. In her state she pushed through the crowds thinking if she could only touch the hem of His garment, she would be healed. She pushed though. She lunged out and grabbed the end. At that moment Jesus knew someone had touched Him. He stopped and asked who had touched Him because He felt the power go out of Him. That is what intercession is like. It is giving everything you have to the cause, with no fanfare, no one watching, no one necessarily knowing, as it should be. Then you spend yourself. You move in His power and then when you are finished you realized you are drained.

Praise!

Soon after starting at the church that had the luncheons and the shelter, etc., I was in services and the pastor was standing a couple rows before me. At the end of the praise and worship portion, he turned to me and pointed and said, "You know you're supposed to be on the praise and worship team!" He startled me. I think I jumped a little. I imagine I looked like deer in headlights! Suddenly a huge anxiety overwhelmed me. See, I love to sing. By then I just had a hard time doing in front of anyone but my kids.

The truth was, God already kept giving me the same idea. I was just kind-of brushing the thought and the feeling aside. I was afraid. When my pastor said that out loud, whether he knew or not, it was like God correcting me. I knew it. I felt it! So, when he asked me to at least stop in on a praise and worship practice, I agreed.

When I met with the team, it was a slow start for me, but by the end I was joining in as if I had been there all along. It fit me, or I fit it. It was like putting on a shoe that fits every curve of your foot perfectly. I left that night knowing that was what I was supposed to do.

So, for six and a half years I went from closing my eyes tightly and having God just get me through it, to standing before the throne of God with eyes open wide. One of my most God-fearing, God-celebrating moments I ever had to date, was singing a song I had sang many times, "Finally, I Surrender," by Misty Edwards. I must have closed my eyes briefly, and when I opened them, my youngest daughter was standing on the floor in front of me looking up and about a hundred people had their arms raised praising God with everything they had. No matter what has escaped my memory since then, that never has and likely never will. When God moved me out of doing that corporately, it felt like a good part of me was cut off. The reality is, it just felt like it because it had become such a big part of my life.

I do still worship Him in song and other ways all the time. Worship is a way of life, not sets of songs anyway.

VISIONS

Though earlier I talked about being able to "see," I wanted to just hit the highlights here again, before we venture on to a few things He has shown me. Prior to seeing all the time and still now from time to time, I had or have visions. Before I had many more God dreams. All these years later, dreams and visions seem to have switched places. I see them in snaps, like seconds, and sometimes longer, where I can take in the details a little more.

Visions seem curiously surprising to me still. They happen occasionally, and seem to have no warning before or much explanation after. Then as I bring it to God, He will work me through what I have seen. Sometimes, every now and again there will be a very clear, very highlighted one that seems to last for some time. Generally, at least for me, they are more warning visions. They are also more about some world, but mostly national events to come. They are hard to deal with, hard to see, hard to think about, and even harder to speak. To be honest, they are the type of calamities the prophets in the bible had to relay. To repeat a phrase I learned from my husband and our friends, "It is what it is."

To end this portion, I never asked for this. It is hard to muster the courage to tell a soul, and even where you do, they often scoff or make fun of you. Worse, many just chalk it up to you being crazy. It took me awhile to get over that part. Now I guess, I choose to be who God made me, period.

CHAPTER EIGHT

Utterances, Words & Visions

Just as in the bible Jesus never healed a person the same way, the Lord also rarely tells or shows people things the same way either. He might give me a vision but give my friend a dream and give a neighbor a word, yet still relay the same message. Certain messages might be given to selected ones that He has ordained to carry to the masses because He made them, formed them and groomed them to be able to. It isn't anything great about the messenger, except perhaps they said yes and then was obedient with that which He gave them to do.

People also receive personal messages. It could be about something they need to do, need to stop doing, something He is calling them to, a circumstance, or others close to them.

Sometimes He will send a person to another and often He won't. It is not for the one that receives to know why, although I have found, He does not mind if you ask.

I know before I write this next part, I might take flak from some that do believe but will not agree with these statements. The Lord can speak to whomever He wants. He can speak to and show things to people who do not yet even know Him. How? He's God. Why? He loves them and wants them to know Him. I'm not going to argue about this. I won't have a debate about this with anyone. Why? It is hard to refute when you have had a personal experience.

He is no respecter of persons. He did it for me when I did not know Him at all. He also did it for me when I had known Him, but went back into the world and was not living my commitment to Him various times. He will do it for any other person in the whole world. His arm is not too short to reach all in the world, whether religious or not, and whether any religion they had, believed in Him or not. People make religion. God is God, Creator over all, and He longs for all to come to Him.

Over my life, I have been told or shown many things. Much of what I have seen has not occurred yet. However, I feel it is all very close. Perhaps the clue to that lies with Him stressing that I would be a prophet for the "end times." However, even large, cataclysmic things might be a "know this," and not a "tell this, for at least a time. There are some things I have seen that are only now likely going to be said by me here, and others that will be withheld.

I only know of two He has said will be in this book, though He eluded we may add a few as we go. With that, let's proceed.

Fire Anointing & Warning – January 21, 2018

"I am bringing an offering. I am bringing an anointing of fire to My church, to My people."

Then He made me know that he was bringing this fire anointing to anyone that believes, whether currently running for Him, sleeping or prodigal. For those that are not familiar with those terms, by sleeping He simply meant not focusing or seeking Him anymore, rather like having been lulled to sleep, and therefore inactive. By prodigal, He means people who have known Him but chose to run after things in the world and have turned their back on Him and went about their own way.

"I am coming and bringing great manifestations with the fire."

He then asked me if I remembered when I first asked Him (Jesus) into my heart, and I said yes. Then I saw a picture of me standing as a fifteen-year-old girl. He reminded me of the tongues trailing out. He stated, but with a question, "That was great, right?" Again, I answered, "Yes." So then repeated:

"I am bringing great manifestations with the fire."

Then He quoted part of John 14:12. He said: *"See these things I do, these and these and greater you shall do."* Then He asked me, "Remember, I brought Lazarus out of the tomb?"

Just as I started to answer and say, "Wow, what's greater than bringing the dead back to life?" He interrupted me.

"But I am bringing a sword."

As He said the words I "saw" a huge sword come down. Then He continued saying that He was bringing the sword down into the center of His church. He quoted the scripture about separating the bone and marrow. *"For the word of God is living and powerful, and sharper than any two-edged sword piercing even to the division of soul and spirit, and of joints and marrow, and is a discerner of thoughts and intents of the heart."* Hebrews 4:12 NKJV. He continued, stating:

"For those that accept the anointing, they will be as fireballs. Like fireballs, they will move forward in formation with great manifestations following."

While He said those words, I saw silver balls, like one would see in a pinball machine.

They were rolling forward in perfect formation, as military jets or birds do. They appeared as 6-10. I am sorry, it was a lot to hear and see all at once!

Then I saw them again, and there was brilliant indigo and white-colored flames coming from these balls. It was beautiful and powerful. Then He finished:

"As for the Lukewarm, if they choose to remain lukewarm, then they will be cut off."

At that, my heart was hit hard, and He stopped talking. I struggled with the last part because I knew many riding the fence between standing in and for the kingdom, or in and for the world. I mean, I'd done it myself! I also knew many that did not know Him at all! Sadly, I still do.

The fear of God was all over me! I always have it, but I think He wanted me to know how serious this all was, and that He meant what He said. He did not say "cut-off" forever to me, but also did not say they weren't. I know Revelation 3:15-16 NKJV says: "I know your works, that you are neither cold or hot. I wish you were cold or hot. So then because you are lukewarm, and neither cold or hot, I will vomit you out of My mouth." I will leave that for you to seek out with Him. So, the entirety of the spoken word was:

"I am bringing an offering. I am bringing an anointing of fire to My church, to My people.

I am coming and bringing great manifestations with the fire.

I am bringing great manifestations with the fire.

But I am bringing a sword.

For those that accept the anointing, they will be as fireballs. Like fireballs, they will move forward in formation with great manifestations following.

As for the Lukewarm, if they choose to remain lukewarm, then they will be cut off."

As just some ending thoughts on this Word, I received the Word and visions of this January 21st of 2018. Since that time, I have only relayed it to a couple of close friends that also believe, my pastor at that time, and a little later a social media channel that He led me to start.

When delivering to the pastor, I had some weird manifestation myself, almost like an earthquake happening inside and outside my own body. My voice came out shaking, but loud and strong, but I could not control the shaking. In fact, I had a friend grab me under one arm to keep me from falling over.

The moment the word was out, the intense shaking stopped as if it had never happened at all. Though I've had many different manifestations before, I had never had one quite like this or as strong.

I believe this word was given to give knowledge and warning to His church. His heart is to gather those that will be His, that do not know Him yet. He graciously announced that He will be offering a cleansing, so that those of the church can roll like fireballs, together, in one accord, and help Him bring more of His people in. He said those that accepted the cleansing, the Fire Anointing would roll forward with great manifestations following. Though He did not give me a picture of this, He did give me thoughts of the casting out of demons, laying hands on the sick and seeing them recover, blind eyes opening, legs growing out, and the dead coming back to life.

Perhaps not the moment I had the word and visions, but after I relayed it all to the pastor later that morning, it occurred to me that God was not just telling me of the fire anointing. He wasn't just telling me of the fireballs that would roll in unison with His great power and authority to gather His people either. He was asking me if I wanted it. Many times, He talks to me and states things using questions, I believe this was one of those times. He was saying, "This is what I am doing. Daughter, here it is."

I knew the cleansing was coming. Even outside the word which says so, and states the church is first, He had been showing me things connected to it from at least July of 2017. Seven months I had been shown people being let down into the water, covered in water, and on scales. In fact, scales were shown over and over, repeatedly. I'd seen myself on the scales, my husband on the scales, various friends, and family on the scales, and just loads of people in general. Each time I prayed and cried out to God. I also plead the blood of Christ for all that I saw.

I had no grid or set of instructions. It is, however, what I did. Some might argue why would God give such an important

word to some unknown person that does not have a huge plat-
form to deliver it. I guess I would answer, I don't know either.
He just did.

CHAPTER NINE
Small Glimpses Still Have Meaning

Sometimes when talking to people they think that the large dreams or visions with lots of details are more important than the small visions or the snap pictures. I disagree. I think that everything God chooses to share is for a reason; therefore, it's all-important. Also, I've found though something might seem simplistic, much can be packed into that small thing. Therefore, I am going to relay some short visions or dreams and explain what God told me they meant.

They Are Waiting

I saw myself portrayed as almost outlined, like a simple realistic cartoon with only black and white hues. I was in the water. It almost looked like a cove, and I was moving forward, nearing huge wooden double doors in the rock that were rising as a backdrop. As I moved closer still, I saw that the water was noticeably deeper. When I got to the front of the doors, it was at the top of my neck. I looked up and realized that big locks held chains that were holding the doors shut. The moment I saw it, it was as if an invisible hand unlocked the locks and they came off. The doors opened and on the other side, and in the water, were hundreds, maybe thousands of people. They were just on the other side, waiting to get in.

Even though the doors were now open, they still could not come in because there were barriers between them and the doors, protruding out of the water on their side. The looks were highlighted on their faces. They looked weary, sad, almost desperate. I don't remember a sound, yet I know that I was moved away from the door. Then I was brought back a little more and a little more. It was as if I was only supposed to see that they were waiting, just on the other side.

The vision ended and then in my mind's ear, the vision was being explained: I was in the water because I was already in the Kingdom and I had been being cleansed. I was moving further into the water because I had gone deeper and deeper with God. I was directed to go to the doors, but until I got to a deep place with God, the doors were locked to me. Once I got there, the locks were removed. The people on the other side were unsaved of the world that will be ushered into the Kingdom. Even with the doors open to them, they still couldn't come because they still have barriers. These could be anything, but likely mostly unbelief, or things they put in front of themselves that keep them from God. The doors were left wide open. They will be ushered into the Kingdom.

God was speaking of an upcoming time when a great many people will come to the Kingdom pretty much at once, due to the great outpouring. He wants His that are in the Kingdom already, to be willing to jump in and help Him usher in the great number.

Then there was a warning. I was told those not ready to jump in would be left waiting on the sidelines, basically watching the ones who were ready to help God bring in this harvest of souls. They would also be waiting to be re-ushered in. The re-ushered tells me, that those folks that weren't ready to help, likely would need to repent.

Dead in the Water

I cannot tell you how many times I have seen people dead in the water! It seems like you could not have multiple reasons to see dead people in various bodies of water, but I can tell you, He has spoken to me about several different things this way. Each time it seemed to mean something different. Today, we will focus on the one He brought to my mind. Perhaps at a point in the future, the others will be described.

This time it was as if I was standing at a bay area. It seemed like nighttime. I was not seeing myself. I was seeing out of my eyes. Suddenly, I saw the water had risen. It came rolling in. I saw things in the water. I thought they were boards. Then one bobbed up a bit and I saw it was a person's body! The person's face was not highlighted. Then there was another body and another.

I watched with breath paused for a moment, wondering if whatever this was could be avoided, but got no answer. Then I saw a highlight on one, like a flashlight shining, and she got up. Then a man stood up and walked out of the water, and so on. Then it just ended as quickly as it came.

The interpretation I was given was we are in dark times. Many people are "dead in the water," because they do not know Jesus. If they do not know Jesus, they cannot be reconciled to God. However, God has a plan, a great outpouring of His love and spirit, where He plans to bring many who are currently spiritually dead to be "alive" in Him. Simply, God showed me that He is going to bring others into the Kingdom that right now are "dead in the water."

The Train (Approx. February 2017)

Before I tell you about "The Train," I must explain that this one should be read carefully, and if you choose to only pay attention to one thing in this book, I pray it is this vision. For whatever reason, when I was led to start a channel on a social media venue, except for an introduction, this was the first one He told me to put on it. When He talked to me about this book and I asked if any of the prophecies or visions would be in, He said yes. Then this was the first one He named would go in. Then later it was given as the last position, making it apparent that He wants it to be some of the ending thoughts.

Truly, I have no idea exactly when it started, but for months before getting a word about it I would "see" a train. The first time it appeared I was standing in worship service at the church I went to at that time. Months went by, maybe even a year, and I would often see that train. For a while, it was always the same. I saw the Lion of Judah driving the train. He appeared as an actual lion, upright, driving the train from the Engineer's position. He was driving, and I always saw a train with open cars, seats, almost like a train kids ride at a fair.

The first time I saw it, it came from my right going left. That time I saw it at a slight distance. The cars were full of people, most sitting, with a few standing up. The people seemed to be all ages and nationalities. Their wardrobe was a wide array. There seemed to be all the socio-economic classes included, from ones in suits to one's that looked like they might have been homeless for a long time. One particularly was highlighted.

My vision was taken in to see the young man closely. He was standing. He was young. He had short hair that partially stood up like a wave toward the front and one side, and he was riddled with visible tattoos and a few piercings. That was the first time I saw the train, but overall, I think the way I saw the vision the first time is what holds what He wanted to say.

After seeing the Lion of Judah driving the train many times, sometimes He would give me a part or piece. When He did, it would be based on the original time I saw it.

Eventually, I felt I knew what all the first vision meant. Then, He changed it. He started alternating between the Lion of Judah driving the train full of people, and my husband driving a motorcycle with the train cars attached. This went on for a while. Even later, right toward the end, I even was shown myself pulling the train cars with my trike.

Visually, the Lion of Judah was driving a train. He was in the position of Engineer. The train appeared as an open train that kids would ride, yet the riders seemed to be all ages. They also appeared to be from different places geographically and economically. He made sure my mind noted the wide variety of people I saw. These words were spoken to me:

"These are my people. These are those that do not know me, but they will know me. I will lead them out."

The rest He made me know. The train was shown open, like a kid train, because these people will soon be His children. He was the Engineer because He is the ultimate engineer, that knows how to take the people I saw from unbelief to belief. He repeated they were His people, because He wanted everyone to know they come from all parts of the world, are all colors, and from all walks of life. He made certain I saw and could relay everyone does not look as many people expect.

Lastly, I felt His great love for them all, for us all. He showed me in a simple way the harvest of people yet to come. As far as my husband and I, it was symbolic of those He would have us help lead to the Kingdom, and a call I believe he and I have.

CHAPTER TEN

The Supernatural Side of God

I have never been very fond of scary movies. I was usually the one who would tightly close my eyes and block my ears. It's rather ironic I ended up with the gifts I've been given; but I have often seen that God does have a sense of humor.

Now far into having a relationship with the Lord, and knowing more about spiritual things, I, for sure, do not want to watch scary or horror movies anymore. It isn't that I am afraid now.

I "see" too much to be afraid. It's because I know it opens doors, spiritual doors.

I have come to believe that much of the reason there is so much interest in things of the occult, witchcraft, mysticism, magic, and even shows or movies with demons or zombies, is because we were made after our Father in heaven. He is supernatural. So, if we lack a relationship with Him, we have a place within us never truly satisfied.

Some people refer to it as a "God-shaped" hole. I agree. I had it. Adding to this, being fashioned after a supernatural father, but not having the supernatural either, would make one curious or yearning for something they didn't even know they were missing.

Keeping that in mind, not all believers see and not all believers even hear, although I think they might, and just don't understand it's God. Not all are given the task to relay words or visions, but everyone is given gifts, everyone. I believe that gifts are given that will be needful or helpful for the path He will lead you to, and for the tasks, He will have for you to do on earth. Sometimes new gifts emerge. This has everything to do with obedience to what He asked you to do before, because this new thing will be needed, or just out of His good pleasure. Yes, He does sometimes do things just because, and sometimes it's even because we ask. It has nothing to do with you being more loved than the next person who believes, because He loves us all, including all those who do not yet believe.

To be honest, sometimes, especially when first getting my bearings, some of all of this has been excruciating. Some things I have been made to see felt as if it drained the life from me.

Still, when my spiritual sight was off, I was suddenly mortified that perhaps I had failed something or He did not need me in this way any longer. Maybe He had to allow that so that I could feel my real heart for the gifts He gave me. After all, prophets in the bible were always sent to tell people what would take place, and often it came in the form of warnings. Maybe I had to learn to stand in the heaviness, so that I would stand, with Him, and become who I was created to be.

Know this, more important than any person, angel, demonic realm, the heavenly hosts and the clouds of witnesses, or any piece or part of a supernatural life, even where supernatural is more normal than the normal, is Him, period. Don't lose sight of that part. Gifts are to be used in walking with Him for the Kingdom, that's it. They assist us in completing our missions here, which when we accept, might be the toughest jobs we'll come to love. Then, come hell and high water, you will do whatever you have to, for as long as you must, because by then, your heart has changed. Likely your love has changed as well.

I wondered as this book came to the prophetic part, how He would sew it all up. At first, I was surprised considering the stunning and sometimes cataclysmic things I have seen that He would leave all of that out. Eventually, the theme did emerge though. He showed His intent to show Himself and let people know that He truly loves them. I think secondary to that fact,

He wanted to reach out to believers and non-believers. He

wanted to show that there is certainly, more than meets the eye!

Still, in closing, I need to state that I have seen many things which are coming in this world. While some might be interceded for, it will not change all that is coming. Wars, wars and rumors of wars, hasn't that been our whole lifetime? Yet, there will be war. Natural disasters have also come and gone, and people grieved and went on. Yet more will come that this world has never seen! Hearts will grow even colder and harder, and people will be enticed to turn on their mothers, fathers, sisters, brothers, and friends, sometimes from desperation, other times out of hatred.

I liken it to a great movie, with many spine-tingling climactic events and cliff hangers, whose ending is told at the beginning. Then you watch the whole thing to see how they got there in the first place. So, here we all are, walking it out.

For those that do not know Him, I hope you find Him soon. In my heart, and I believe in God's, this book is for you most of all! Jesus truly is Lord. He is the way to be reconciled to God. God is not looking for perfect. He is simply looking for willing. I promise you.

The seen and unseen are colliding in the spirit and physical, and things are coming, soon.

.

TAKE HEED!

But concerning the times and the seasons, brothers, you have no need that I should write to you. For you yourselves know perfectly that the day of the Lord so comes as the thief in the night. For when they say, 'Peace and safety!' 'then sudden destruction comes upon them, as labor pains upon a pregnant woman. And they shall not escape. But you brothers, are not in darkness, so that this day should overtake you as a thief.
—I Thessalonians 5:1-4 NKJV

ABOOKS

ALIVE Book Publishing and ALIVE Publishing Group
are imprints of Advanced Publishing LLC,
3200 A Danville Blvd., Suite 204, Alamo, California 94507

Telephone: 925.837.7303
alivebookpublishing.com

www.ingramcontent.com/pod-product-compliance
Lightning Source LLC
LaVergne TN
LVHW011412080426
835511LV00005B/508